RUBANK
Treasures
for OBOE

Printable Piano Accompaniments

PLAYBACK+
Speed • Pitch • Balance • Loop

CONTENTS

To access recordings and PDF piano accompaniments, go to:
www.halleonard.com/mylibrary

Enter Code
2095-3456-8636-1160

ISBN 978-1-4803-5241-4

RUBANK®

HAL•LEONARD®

7777 W. BLUEMOUND RD. P.O. BOX 13819 MILWAUKEE, WI 53213

Copyright ©2018 by HAL LEONARD CORPORATION
International Copyright Secured   All Rights Reserved

Visit Hal Leonard Online at
www.halleonard.com

Siciliana

Oboe

G.B. Pergolesi
Arranged by Clair W. Johnson

Andante cantabile

(5)

(9)

(13)

(17)

(23)

(27)

(31)

00121402

Gavotte

Oboe

François Joseph Gossec
Arranged by Clair W. Johnson

00121402

Solvejg's Song
from *Peer Gynt Suite No. 2*

Oboe

Edvard Grieg
Arranged by Clair W. Johnson

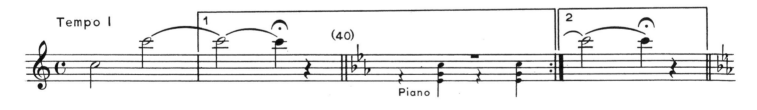

6

Sarabanda and Rigaudon

Oboe

I – Sarabanda

Arcangelo Corelli
Transcribed by H. Voxman

II – Rigaudon

George Frideric Handel
Transcribed by H. Voxman

poco rit. on repeat

Chansonette

Oboe

A.M. Barret
Arranged by A.W. Pazemis

On Quiet Waters

Oboe

Paul Koepke

Bourrée and Menuet
from Flute Sonata No. III

Oboe

George Frideric Handel
Edited by H. Voxman

Crépuscule
(Twilight)

Oboe

Gabriel Parès
Transcribed by R.A. Judy

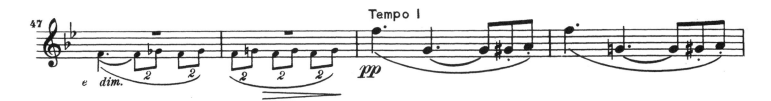

Pastorale
from Concerto for Oboe

Oboe

Ludwig F.W. Klemcke
Edited by H. Voxman

Danse Arabe

from *The Nutcracker Suite*

Oboe

P.I. Tchaikovsky
Arranged by Clarence E. Hurrell

00121402

15

✳ Forked F fingering may be used here.

00121402

Allegro Moderato
from Trio No. 1 ("London")

Oboe

Franz Joseph Haydn
Adapted by R. Hervig

Aria and Dance

Oboe

Leroy Ostransky

Allegro vivace (♩. = 116)

Lamento
(Nocturne)

Oboe

Luigi Bassi
Edited by H. Voxman

First Concertino

Oboe

Georges Guilhaud
Edited by H. Voxman

* Designates a recording "click" (accomp. recording only)

† Three fast clicks here anticipate the triplet rhythm in the piano accompaniment at *a tempo*.